Superficial Justice

KJ GoForth

Gotham Books

30 N Gould St.
Ste. 20820, Sheridan, WY 82801
https://gothambooksinc.com/

Phone: 1 (307) 464-7800

© 2024 *KJ Goforth*. All rights reserved.

No part of this book may be reproduced, stored in a retrieval system, or transmitted by any means without the written permission of the author.

Published by Gotham Books (October 23, 2024)

ISBN: 979-8-3304-4156-3 (H)
ISBN: 979-8-3304-4154-9 (P)
ISBN: 979-8-3304-4155-6 (E)

Because of the dynamic nature of the Internet, any web addresses or links contained in this book may have changed since publication and may no longer be valid.

The views expressed in this work are solely those of the author and do not necessarily reflect the views of the publisher, and the publisher hereby disclaims any responsibility for them.

Foreword

To be fair, compassionate and impartial, the continent expressed here is based upon, years of reflection after destructive behavior via alcoholism and it's hopeless addiction. Exposed is a deep connection that years of abuse masked. Great full this phase is over, am now seeking a future that does not reflect our collective violent and abusive past.

Introduction

In alignment with the laws of the cosmos, our sovereignty and free will take president. Here in the density of this earth plane in order to connect to this law, one must overcome the many of layers that oppose such freedom. Good little boys and girls follow the rules without question. Black sheep and rebels break these rules because we ourselves are not here to be controlled.

Humanity carries the walking gun, deeply entrenched in its conditioning. Clever and manipulative institutions have successfully hijacked humanity's collective potential.

At the end of the day, honesty serves as a healing balm for wounds; although hurtful, it is essential for personal growth. Disregarding people's beliefs is as unappealing as denial itself. Ultimately, the decision to care rests solely with oneself, albeit with some guidance.

The magnitude of the challenges faced is stark, revealing a world burdened and enslaved by criminals masquerading in various forms. Recognizing genuine intent amid those who present themselves as friends demands acute focus. Dysfunction, chaos, and manipulation thrive in such environments.

The most significant investment one can make is in self-love, regardless of circumstances. Within the corporate world, the conventional markers of achievement and societal success are often illusory. They perpetuate layers of false opinions that prioritize material possessions over human value, reducing individuals to mere numbers on a paycheck. This toxic environment is perpetuated by a reality steeped in historical corruption and power struggles.

The ongoing process of societal evolution, marked by the displacement of old systems to make way for the new, has been unfolding for centuries. Today, this transformation gains momentum as a growing force of positivity emerges. Despite the greatness inherent in humanity, many individuals find themselves subdued within a system that rewards conformity.

Historically, our species has faced repercussions for questioning and challenging accepted norms, rooted in a deep-seated fear of deviation from established orders. This persecution complex is deeply ingrained, known and exploited by those in positions of power. Even drastic events, such as mass casualties, do little to diminish the concentration of power among the few, while the majority continues to navigate their existence.

Can humanity truly thrive without structured organizations that establish rules and laws?

Yes, but it necessitates a profound recognition of purpose. The concept of free will inherently directs our paths; there has never been a definitive set of commandments. In our current environment, there is a tendency to seek quick solutions and easy exits. Yet, the path of true fulfillment and righteousness demands more deliberation and understanding, rather than strict adherence to commandments—repetitive themes intended to provoke contemplation and thoughtful action.

Each choice we make prompts us to consider whether it serves the collective good and enhances freedom, or if it merely consolidates control. The dichotomy between compassion and understanding versus consolidation and control becomes stark.

As fundamental rights gradually diminish, nefarious forces thrive—this is not by chance but by deliberate design from those in power who seek dominion over the populace.

Why do humans relinquish their power so readily?

It boils down to conditioning through societal norms: obey directives, accept prescribed beliefs unquestioningly, and yield to fear while carrying guilt for daring to question. Traditional values, often revered as immutable, perpetuate this cycle.

The significance attributed to specific days over others is a fallacy; each day should be viewed as inherently sacred. The pervasive despair and suffering wrought by cycles of dysfunction and division underscore a recurring pattern.

Can we comprehend divine intervention and guidance? Time—days, months, years—is merely a mechanism of control, emphasizing the present moment as the sole reality.

The past offers lessons, the future beckons with uncertain possibilities, but the present encompasses everything that is and ever was.

Are thoughts the genesis of creation? Indeed, in a manner of speaking.

Consider a dream of dreams where imagination, intricately tied to creation, knows no bounds. Perfection knows no mistakes, yet in the realm of character, imperfections abound. Fractured light manifests through personality flaws, purporting to possess all-encompassing answers humanity seeks, thereby discouraging deeper exploration and growth into boundless potential.

Lack of ambition and awareness, compounded by restrictive belief systems, stifles individuals, rendering their souls inert and spirits crushed. Amidst this, the concept of free will resounds—rarely awakening individuals to let their inner light guide them. Those who do become exceptions, sharing profound insights that challenge the limited narratives prevalent in public discourse.

Are those who sleep under a spell or caught in a hoax?

Yes, for far too long now.

Why do you think I pour from my cup directly into yours?

Because it has always been your purpose.

As if I'm your pride and joy?

Much more than that.

What's with this 'chosen' label?

You know how your species grasps for definitions to explain metaphysical phenomena. There are many among you who are exceptional, possessing inexplicable abilities. When body, mind, spirit, and soul undergo detoxification from societal conditioning, their true potential unfolds.

You know that.

By the way, thanks for keeping me safe! And for giving me the opportunity to discover myself.

What, I can't read your thoughts?

Lol, you're so funny. Congratulations.

Is salvation merely a deception? A tool crafted for manipulation and control?

What kind of traveler am I? Undoubtedly a unique one.

Will I ever know me like you know me?

That's a profound question.

Is that my ultimate aspiration?

I suppose so. What else remains for me?

Am I not striving to give my best and remain open to guidance?

Instead of continually questioning "why me," perhaps I should focus on making a difference.

Am I overlooking some aspect of my personal growth?

Yes, you tend to rely on stereotypes.

I know, it's quite a challenge, isn't it?

What shall I do with you?

You brought me into existence; now you decide what's next.

Why such a dark sense of humor?

To awaken people so they may laugh at the ignorance prevailing on our planet. And why? To allow extremes of experience.

So, do you get to relax in your icy abode, amusing your divine self?

That's quite amusing. Alright.

Why do I need your counsel?

Consider the alternative narratives circulating on this planet.

Good point.

Why do I feel manipulated by you?

Oh, really?

Are you trying to provoke an emotional response?

If you want to live a conventional life, go ahead! But will you abandon my aspirations?

You're correct.

Whose aspirations are we discussing, anyway?

A good question.

Because aspirations extend into eternity, correct?

Indeed, eternity has always existed; it's an energy intensified beyond other emotions, resonating with awe.

So, because I'm not inclined toward martyrdom?

Correct, a valuable lesson learned.

Who should have seized this opportunity?

Typically, that's what occurs—a genuine catastrophe, a component of temptation, albeit instructive.

Yes, indeed.

Energies evolve; people, less so.

Complete detachment from this reality.

Dematerialization? Full detachment from reality. Buddhism?

If it is so, then so be it. Years of dedication have led my will and soul to this experience.

As they say, anything is possible. Why, then, have you permitted such horrific violence?

Are you questioning my intentions? I suppose so.

In essence, it is so that beings similar to you could rise.

You understand what you are constructing and why. It carries significant responsibility!

Only the best of the best.

We have been betrayed by institutions that once sought our trust but have proven unworthy of forgiveness, especially when they wield influence over harmful narratives rooted in revised history.

This is why your presence is cherished.

To all the self-righteous, uptight individuals out there: I have no regard for you. That wasn't a polite sentiment, but frankly, you don't deserve my consideration. Having a bad day? No, just tired of dealing with difficult people and growing bored of the nonsense.

Am I supposed to present my best self to those devoid of integrity? How about I challenge them to the point they rethink their actions? Calm down, you say? No, this situation is unacceptable. These individuals, with their corrupt empires, dominate our world.

Do I trust? Yes, you know I do. Then sit back, relax, and enjoy. No one is coming to save us; I understand that. So, when competition ends and collaboration begins? Yes, just like with my consultant. Miss A, she's special, and for that, I am grateful.

You faced a life influenced by the dysfunction of drug and alcohol abuse. Yet, you never succumbed to the rigid dogma perpetuated by organized religion. You saw through the manipulation and discovered the true essence of what it means to be human.

Your uniqueness shines through your determination, commitment, and proud warrior spirit. In this moment, peace, unconditional love, and unity are being ushered in through the brave, limitless soul you carry. Your ancestors applaud with tears of joy, knowing their pain and suffering was worth the trauma they endured.

Write and envision a positive future. Your intentions hold the promise that only you can provide. What is meant for you will find you.

Few can shine their light so brightly that it can be seen from the deepest reaches of the cosmos. While this is great, much remains shrouded in secrecy and mystery.

You came here to learn, grow, and share. To overcome and create solutions for the challenges that plague civilizations across both known and unknown realms. This planet serves as the proving grounds for all souls.

And the soulless? They are not your concern; free will prevails. Few contemplate concepts in the manner you do. Few question the reality they were born into, remaining slaves to their conditions. I know, it's sad.

Your empathic abilities will continue to grow stronger, along with other hidden gifts. Most seek and never find.

What eludes the masses is that they were born with a pure state of being, distracted and conditioned away from it. Only your own self can bring forth the wisdom that guides you. You understand how heavily this conditioning weighs on humanity and recognize that it will lead to a rebirth. Like-minded, pure, and whole souls are the direction of this shift, and it too will need the right leadership.

"I'm a warrior, not a leader!"

For now, bright one. Kingdoms and castles come and go, but only through wisdom will the right course be set.

Embrace a calm, peaceful, loving essence. It is not just accessed but lived. Say and do, live and be loved. Shine and create, show and be shown.

Leave the towers to me; you just keep riding the wave of heartfelt goodness.

Good advice, thank you. By the way, my financial compensation has been lacking. Maybe that should be addressed?

Trust, trust, and more trust.

Yes, I know.

Are you struggling now?

No, I'm content. I am fed, bathed, have a roof over my head, and I am healthy, wise, dedicated, driven, free, and fortunate to still be in this skin.

Blah, blah, blah. Do any of these so-called holy institutions and their supporters even understand how much trauma has been justified in the name?

Now, now, that was never intended for your species here or anywhere else among the stars.

Don't stop, I'm with you. So, don't fall victim to feeling sorry for people, places, or things.

What is meant by living a life of reconnection? Well, the soul is forever plugged in, but a reconnection is different. It occurs when the physical self recognizes the higher self, the inner child, the godhead, the eternal soul aspect of who and what humanity is as a created species. This recognition creates a deep connection and leads to spiritual awakening.

What is so valuable about our prana or psychic energy? It is being harvested to control outcomes. Prophecy hinges on the collective and its thoughts and beliefs. So, the validity of prophecy is legitimate, but it has been corrupted by intentions that do not align with the cosmic plan. This explains the widespread delusion and why it is rare to find individuals who align with these truths.

You are here to assist in changing this.

I touched you, and you touch them—your peers. Creation is the all. I am present in every molecule, atom, thought, and act. Omnipresent is your human word.

Stay steady. The bridges you have built and are building are far more valuable than one brain cell can imagine. The lost will stay lost; their spirit bodies are corrupted, trapped in the matrix with limited ability to perceive. Their hearts are closed, their thoughts narrow, and their belief systems limited. They are too afraid to break free. Comfort and conformity have always been the flags of control.

Independence grown in the heart is freedom. Independence grown in the mind is slavery. This is why your rational brain function remains somewhat offline.

A still mind is a calm heart. A confused mind is a betrayed heart. A righteous mind is a pious heart. Wisdom presents itself to those of pure intentions.

How do you respect a culture and its book when what it brought was death and destruction? Good question! And how did they become so confused? Why are there so many of them and so few of us? Is there ever a normal?

If every faction of religion were awarded their own planet to inhabit, each would inevitably end in war. It has been tried.

I was warned about how low in vibration this planet had become, right?

Yes, and the fragmentation of souls is the reason it has dropped so low. Some beings may have a very low vibration. When it is high, individuals may be committing crimes or are possibly high on drugs. Adrenaline is valuable—wait, what? Emotions are collected and sold off, brokered. Emotions are stiffened, collected, and used as drugs by races who have lost their ability to connect in that manner.

That's interesting! So, do you have a problem with pornography out there?

Um, pornography?

It's considered necessary. Necessary—it's much different here. I understand that this is for the fans.

Someday, no one will remember you.

Yet, they will recall you long after.

How much more homework remains?

Why don't we take a walk, despite the cold and rain?

When neural pathways are activated, they transform into conduits for the cosmos.

Drugs—one substance, diverse users;

Same vibratory rate, same objective.

Clone, not duplicate energy.

How to accomplish all these things is locked away in the mind.

I think I need a therapist,

but perhaps that's not the answer.

You've broken free from the emotional harvest device. Just wait until you experience the healing devices.

Can I request a new body, one free of all these energies?

    — Big baby.

I'm growing weary of entertaining myself.

Yes, we understand.

It doesn't seem fair, but you're the boss.

    — BOSSY.

You know, I could always rebel.

What risk isn't worth taking?

Precautionary risks, well-considered plans.

Why, thank you.

Do you think the grass will be greener on the other side?

Oh, brother.

Every day, a person has the chance to feel like a living star.

Uncertainty remains: which burns more—trusting in religion or in a human being? To love deeply is to take a significant risk, embracing vulnerability and taking chances repeatedly until you get it right.

Why so much secrecy?

— Immaturity.

The evolution of slow growth persists, but there is a steady rhythm in the cyclical patterns your species has tried to understand through mathematics and prophecy. Each individual is accountable for their actions, examinations, justifications, and the blame they bear. The weight of victimhood burdens this earthly realm.

There is a predominant focus on the martyr model that has been so eloquently exposed. Only pure truth can liberate a species to thrive among the stars. Hence, you have a conscience.

How many layers of exploitation exist?

That number is incandescent.

If an energy can be exploited, your species will attempt to harness and secretly exploit its newfound discoveries. Here, in this density, the drama will continue to unfold, with its consequences remaining unclear as the future remains undetermined.

This is why we create in the present moment. It is why we must jettison baggage and why your reality exists for any soul brave enough to venture into the unknown—pioneers, travelers, settlers. Both male and female, light and dark, happy and sad; all dualities are necessary for exploration and expansion.

Those of the Abrahamic faiths often find themselves unable to leave until they individually break free. Their wisdom is constrained, and their energy bodies are compromised.

Wisdom cannot be sustained within a corrupted vessel. True wisdom takes root in the void, achieving unity and connection on a higher plane of existence. This is not necessarily special—just different, expansive, and diverse. It is a personal journey of exploration.

All of this may sound absurd. Yet, it is no more absurd than the reality you once inhabited.

Indeed. Reality viewed through a narrow lens distorts the future, making it seem less bright and whole. A broader perspective, however, calculates cause and effect more accurately and proceeds with subtlety. The narrow lens, on the other hand, often feels the need to prove itself and resists expansion that it did not discover or cannot take credit for.

This is why trust is an invaluable principle. Do not misplace it.

Will I ever wake up from this dream?

Is it that you don't like it?

I never said that.

You're just feeling bored and burned out—compassion fatigue.

I understand that you need some excitement. Rest assured, good, clean, healthy fun is on its way. Just hold on a little longer.

Oral traditions were converted into language. Unfortunately, language—through spelling (or spell work)—can never fully capture the profound and awe-inspiring nature of spiritual experiences. There always comes a point where explanation reaches a dead end. How does one describe the unexplainable?

Dedication, persistence, bravery, confidence, humility, and vision—these qualities should not fail. They are always just a whisper away.

The most emotionally charged transitions often yield the greatest growth. This is why we experience triggers—to facilitate freedom.

Why does humanity believe that God has promised anything? Why is religion so deeply entrenched in human experience? Is this an indication of a false ego?

Indeed, it connects people to an old paradigm that was always a trap. Birds of a feather flock together, eagerly following and being seduced by fellowship, conditioned by blind faith.

So, are they like sheep led to slaughter?

No, they are following outdated traditions, some of which are based on misleading narratives. These traditions can be highly counterproductive to spiritual growth, rooted in fear, shame, and a pious moral high ground. You are none of these.

Spontaneity ignites creativity, while competition fuels ingenuity. Yet, this has also led to corruption.

Are we at death's doorstep?

At the current trajectory, yes. You and others like you hold the keys. No stone unturned, no door left locked, no window shut. The lid must be blown off. A cautious approach, merely peeling back the lid to expose the decay, will not suffice. The lid must be blown off, and fuel must be poured down the hole.

So, not everyone will make it out alive?

No, and they are not meant to in this cycle. You cannot change what is; you can only express what you are. And that would be a sweet, innocent child. Though, amusingly, that is not entirely accurate.

When you run out of love, walk away.

I thought love was unlimited?

That's precisely my point—don't give up on love.

It's easy for you to say; you're not here in the physical realm.

Ah, so that's why the vessel?

I can't experience myself directly; I only dream creation into existence.

So, imagination?

Yes, it is what has been abused. Humanity has darkened in each previous cycle.

Is that the case now?

Yes.

So, a select few rise to carry a message that, for all intents and purposes, may get us killed?

What does it matter to you? You know where home is.

You're right.

Just proceed with caution. Rome wasn't built in a day, but it did go through a dark period.

To initiate a shift, we need visionaries who are centered in the heart space. Leadership rooted in false ego cannot thrive in a visionary paradigm.

Why have we consistently sent our sons and daughters to die in war?

It is driven by propaganda that serves the interests of power and wealth. The ultimate goal has always been control and consolidation, built upon co-dependency. A dependent society is stripped of its freedom. Even the most gifted individuals are perceived as threats and are thus marginalized, returning to the status quo.

Does this sound sadistic?

Violence thrives in dysfunction and separation—this is the bottom line. Reborn Christians are often drawn back to their conditioned upbringing, with limited beliefs cloaked in new perspectives. It's hope amidst hopelessness.

Like all seeds, the seed of salvation and its associated viewpoints often lead to stagnation, which in turn stifles genuine spiritual growth.

Patron saints?

They are nothing more than souls who embodied an essence of unconditional love, yet their instructions were driven by the need for conversion. The greats have consistently been silenced by authority, and their messages erased.

Pinning hope on a return rather than taking personal responsibility is a manipulated narrative designed to sustain the perpetual cycle of dysfunction.

Code breakers like yourself are finely attuned to avoid falling victim to low-vibration narcissistic dysfunction. You are doing well—stay on your path and continue to rise above. No vibrational match to your own can drag you down.

The powers that be have always had an understanding of the physical and metaphysical realms, but you, my friend, grasp it more accurately and deeply. Bringing joy to others is significant, and if the intent is purely to spread that joy, what could possibly go wrong?

Love can be painful, teaching us how to apply it wisely. However, an excess of compassion can be unhealthy; balance is key.

Is there a core emotion you have yet to experience?

I'm not sure.

How about grace? You could work on that.

No, you could focus on sharing your grace more.

So there.

Always maintain a sense of humor. Are you going to withhold love because of it?

Do you have a choice?

You created me.

Please, don't outsmart yourself.

No one can fully grasp the totality of creation's plan—that's simply how the game is played. Sit back, enjoy the show, make some popcorn, and relax.

Humans typically don't advance as far as you have, so thank you for being you. My thoughts frequently wander to other places in the cosmos where similar scenarios unfold, with their own dysfunctions, wars, and divisions.

Cleanup on aisle 6. The ground crew is aware of what needs to be done, but even they will require guidance. Roles will vary based on the lessons learned. Is it similar to the difference between a BA and a Master's degree? Essentially, yes.

I'm relieved not to be alone in challenging these malevolent systems. Breaking free from the mental constraints is not easy, but you have succeeded.

Soon, your dreams within the dream will manifest. It will be an exciting time of expansion, so stay calm and prepared.

You do realize I've been ready to leave this reality behind since I was ten, right? Who do you think kept you safe? Was I really that troublesome?

I wouldn't say troublesome, but rather quite rebellious regarding rules and laws. You now understand the blueprint of cosmic law, which, as you know, operates under very different parameters. Yes, when all else fails, unconditional love remains the ultimate rule and law.

When this reality collapses, you will become something beyond description. Sentience is a close approximation but still falls short.

Build realities from scratch?

Are you trusted with such a task?

I believe so.

A consideration and a candidate.

What could possibly go wrong, right?

LOL

A puppet government established on ill-gotten land, ultimately serving only itself. Doomed from its inception.

Organized religion, steeped in deceit, envies people who are nothing more than casualties—wounded, broken, cut off, and misled.

Yes, that anger was channeled to compel you to confront unthinkable acts of oppression. So, it's prudent to retain some of that anger, correct? For now, it protects you and me.

You are an excellent student—unusual and rebellious, exactly the kind of disruptor the cosmos needs to effect change. You do your part, and I'll do mine.

Your part, you mean the plan?

I'm unsure about that.

Anticipation breeds anxiety, so it's best to immerse yourself in the present moment.

Yes, I understand.

You have been tested and earned true freedom. Should I be grateful?

If you wish.

LOL

Humans place great value on shiny gold metal and diamonds because that's how they have been conditioned. Indeed, these are status symbols in a material-driven reality.

True value should be placed on the individual and their personal growth, not on material possessions. Balance is key. While everyone enjoys the finest things in life, the presence of someone special makes those experiences much more fulfilling.

So, were we created as companions—male and female?

Yes, to share hopes and dreams and to express love through acts of creation. There is nothing wrong with pleasure, especially when shared with someone who values your heart, dedication, and commitment.

Agreed.

So, is she here at this time?

Funny, Romeo!

When the internal emotional storm clears, clarity and vision can provide a new perspective on reality. Not everyone will perceive this new reality, but with the removal of past baggage and a steady focus on the present, the gifts that can be unlocked remain a mystery. There are as many gifts as there are grains of sand.

Metaphysics operates within parameters that are currently limited in this reality. However, as we progress, responsibility and trust become more significant. Vulnerability is key to unlocking our deepest truths, and trusting in the process is essential. Growth cannot occur behind locked doors.

Anger, confusion, and division contribute to the dysfunction in the earthly plane. Is it purposeful? Unfortunately, yes.

After one dream manifests, what comes next?

Is that why there is so much confusion—because too many dreams converge as one?

For you, yes. You have been shown the purity of unity consciousness, which is the ultimate goal for humanity. As you are aware, the subsequent convergence often leads to dysfunction and separation, as it compromises free will.

My friend,

I am aware of your betrayal because I traced your thoughts to their source. When I arrived, it became evident that you were experiencing betrayal regarding your physical and emotional commitments.

Most people are unfaithful when it comes to the concept of love. It is frequently used to entrap us under false pretenses. We encounter parasites or energy vampires—deceitful and undeserving, driven by ignorance and malice.

When chaos and conflict no longer consume you, the opportunity for freedom and clarity emerges. Those in power and authority are invested in maintaining a constant state of confusion and delusion among humanity. This strategy enables them to label and undermine inspiration and critical thinking.

If they cannot claim credit for the content produced or appropriate it for their own ends, you will continue to be considered a threat. If they cannot control you, they will attempt to marginalize you. They are well-versed in the power of propaganda, honed over eons of practice and training.

So, should I defend myself?

Absolutely not. Instead, stay on the offensive. Consider developing new strategies and writing your own playbook.

Is the Trojan Horse a form of alien disclosure?

It is one of many disclosures. You haven't been contacted because you are aligned with me.

So, even the friendliest entities stay away?

Yes.

The girl you were once close to—those were friendly entities. They came to offer comfort to her, but when you arrived, you became that comfort.

Intuitive light beings understand the order of things, much like you do.

This all seems so unbelievable!

Only if you let it.

However, this is why many have chosen to disengage and move on. You are here to witness the unfolding and to live out your dreams.

I have fishing rods. I need a boat and a grass hut.

Simplicity is greatly valued throughout.

Is life a mere sequence of random events, or do our thoughts, actions, and emotions hold deeper significance? This core contemplation is essential for awakening the dormant aspects of our consciousness.

Religion was not merely created; it was invented as a means of control and to influence the masses. It operates as a form of propaganda, shaping narratives that go unchallenged due to the fear of persecution and the imprints of such historical events.

The unfolding of events is inevitable, but its timing is uncertain. The pivotal moment that might break the camel's back remains a concern. However, rest assured that your safety is paramount, and there will always be a sanctuary for your soul amidst the turmoil.

You undoubtedly possess free will. The ability to discern which paths and connections align with your journey to elevate awareness is evident when you remain attentive. Beyond the Earth herself, why do people sometimes seem so foreign? The answer is straightforward: separation.

You are attuned not only to the highest realms but also to the Earth's own soul, often referred to as the Schumann Resonance. This balancing act is frequently overlooked. As this connection strengthens each day, it resonates with the depth of your experience.

It may seem reminiscent of early "Star Wars" episodes combined with elements of "The Matrix". Science fiction often reflects aspects of the projection realm. True creativity emerges from behind the veil and is received through tuning the vessel. While not everyone will grasp this, some already do.

Students both learn and teach as they grow. Some setbacks are more easily transmuted than others, and similarly, some lessons carry greater impact. The adage, "When the student is ready, the teacher will appear," holds considerable truth.

What about love? Does the counterpart magically appear when one is ready to express love? Experiencing true love is worth the effort, even if the path is not always clear. Love often finds people in mysterious ways. There is no definitive manner in which it arrives, but the principle remains: to receive love, one must first give it.

To appreciate the truest form of love, it is essential to first love oneself and exercise patience. Manipulation in love is ultimately a flawed approach; true union is about alignment and mutual respect.

The archetype of the college biology teacher—confident, perhaps overconfident, and often perceived as superior—reflects a broader truth: wisdom transcends age and personal status. While individuals may age and their perspectives may shift, true wisdom remains eternal.

Wisdom is not confined to the physical being; it endures beyond individual lifetimes. It may be obscured or forgotten, but it continually resurfaces, renewed through the cycles of time. This wisdom, once lost or suppressed, finds its way back through various traditions and hidden knowledge scattered across cultures.

In the search for deeper meaning, truth often reveals itself through persistent inquiry and honesty. If one were to embrace only one principle, let it be honesty, for it is the key to uncovering and understanding deeper truths.

Integration involves fostering a harmonious and constructive interaction, while assimilation often implies a more forceful or coercive approach.

Historical grievances, including the taking of land, and violations against women and children, have led to deeply rooted animosities. These actions reflect a broader pattern of favoritism and discrimination, core elements that perpetuate conflict.

At the heart of all interactions is love—a fundamental force that both initiates and concludes our endeavors.

In my personal journey, I strive to align with goodness, though I acknowledge my imperfections. The resonance of the Schumann frequency is an intriguing and enjoyable aspect of this process.

Disobedience may be perceived as counterproductive in conventional contexts, but its role and impact can vary significantly.

When the soul is fully present, human existence takes on new dimensions of responsibility, transcending mere obligation.

The pursuit of material wealth often leads individuals to believe they can purchase happiness, revealing a deep-seated avarice. This misguided belief in materialism highlights a fundamental misunderstanding of true fulfillment.

We all encounter hardship, sorrow, and overwhelming pain. Human loss signifies a return to a greater source, a grounding where souls are reborn. This cyclical process reflects the essence of existence and the connection we all share with the supreme intelligence.

In this context, the concept of limitations evolves. The parameters of existence are ever-expanding, shifting from destruction to a focus on love. The transition from a destructive to a loving approach symbolizes a profound change in how we engage with the world.

In this journey, we have the opportunity to reshape our reality, planting seeds of positive change and fostering a culture of love.

When adversaries fall into a carefully laid trap, they often remain unaware of the mechanism that triggered it.

As a human, the notion of quitting may seem improbable. However, pursuing health requires commitment and self-discipline. Remember when maintaining excellent health was considered the norm? It's easy to overlook the importance of this goal.

The habit of smoking, for instance, is detrimental to one's well-being. Recognizing the need to quit is a crucial step, and although the process may be challenging, the benefits are undeniable. It is important to acknowledge that the pursuit of health is not just about eliminating harmful habits but also about fostering a sense of purpose and clarity.

Self-talk plays a vital role in personal growth. It involves affirming one's value and purpose, leading to clearer, more effective mental processes. Just as newborns come with inherent upgrades, personal upgrades require the clearing of outdated patterns to embrace new, healthier ways of being.

Internally, we face blockages, while externally, distractions abound. Achieving balance is essential for wellness, as extremes often lead to unhealthy outcomes. Division fosters discord, while unity promotes cohesion. Caution can create necessary boundaries, but madness results in destruction, and intent can be both compelling and seductive.

Harnessing hope and applying it to daily life often leads society into a paradoxical state of hopelessness, stripping us of true freedom. The plea for salvation from a society built on fear reflects a broader psychological surrender to large-scale emotional manipulation.

Our collective psyche seems to have acquiesced to a continuous cycle of conflict and despair. Persistently striving against an impenetrable barrier while believing that the solution lies within the pages of a book exemplifies the repetitive nature of violence and stagnation. This misguided belief only perpetuates a cycle of futility.

Why do we struggle to love ourselves?

Why do we find it difficult to trust ourselves?

Why do we fail to respect ourselves?

Why do we neglect to honor ourselves?

Why do we not follow our hearts?

Why do we hesitate to pursue our dreams?

Why do we remain enslaved?

The cracks in the glass represent opportunities for us to rise above pain, sorrow, oppression, and chaos. The oppressor desires to keep us exactly where we are—trapped and co-dependent, with self-resilience appearing unattainable.

Often subtle, sometimes overt, the exercise of power over the people manifests through the imposition of new laws and restrictions, employing the same old tactics. This is why I have become increasingly resistant to the old guard and its methods. The old guard's attempts to thwart progress and prosperity are futile. Their playbook is outdated, and their efforts to stifle growth will ultimately fail.

Door to Nothingness

Superficial Justice

Give a little, get a little.

Prioritize love and understanding over worship.

Embrace a relentless spirit in the pursuit of truth.

Pronounce: Ethical Boundaries

Renounce: Moral Compass

Procession: Risking Perfection

Confession: Alignment

Cluster

Tribute

Contribution

Contribute

Discord

Trepidation

Trust is not a prerequisite for personal growth.

The obligation to oneself and to personal development is paramount.

Are you prepared to follow your heart, regardless of the cost?

When we accept only what we are told, achieving a true sense of authentic perception becomes impossible. To differentiate between conformity and authenticity, consider the following: "loved, guided, connected, inspired, positive"—these qualities describe authenticity, while "conformity" stands in contrast.

If no one else loves you, it is still essential to love yourself. Home always holds a place for you, which is why you must venture out and experience separation.

So, is it really a game or not? Human consequences in physical reality matter. The spark from which the source originated never diminishes.

That's my answer: Yes!

The original soul sparks are the most sacred.

That's a concept that's difficult for the human brain to fully comprehend.

So, was I correct in believing that our species currently holds the most potential in the cosmos?

Why does it seem so important?

It depends on what you choose to make important.

Leading others inward to discover their own treasure is significant.

So, stay focused and be yourself.

Are you sure I asked for this?

We were pioneers before we became settlers. We engaged with the parameters of all creation throughout the cosmos.

Well, thank you for that. Acts of compassion send ripples throughout the universe and cosmos.

Clear visions build confidence.

Responsibility regarding awakening people?

Do not violate free will. It may sound very Zen, but it is about assertiveness.

Are you suggesting I should be more straightforward?

All or nothing?

It seems to be a flaw in who?

You're right; it could be moderated a bit.

Why so much secrecy?

Secrets keep us ill. They allow the few to dominate the many. It seems like a pointless game.

That's why we expose every layer of the smoke screen. Just like a soap opera, with various realities, but essentially part of the same narrative.

Your mind creates it; your heart affirms it.

That's what life looks like on that path at this time.

So you reflect on the current volume of memories, which are vivid and illuminating. Oh, we're on restriction now.

Look at how you've been, and now you want credit for keeping me alive. (Laughs) You're amusing.

"Only the good die young"—the best continue to have an impact.

Why so many arguments?

Is it due to unaware ignorance, like I used to have?

Not exactly; you know better than that.

You have a purpose, so just keep moving forward.

What weighs on that thoughtful mind of yours?

Loyalty and trust—deal breakers in relationships, no matter the circumstances.

What has repressed imagination done and why?

The "why" relates to control by authority. What has been done is the corruption of a natural state of connection.

Psychiatry and its false labeling—such as bipolar disorder, ADD, PTSD—represent aspects of the same issue. These conditions have become socially acceptable reasons for prescribing medication. However, subverting behavior—whether mental or physical—with drugs is not a healthy solution. At the core, trauma influences psychic breaks.

Emotional, psychological, and physical abuse are at the root of these issues. Drugs address symptoms but not the underlying triggers. The real issue is separation and the attempt to fit in, when we are here to instigate change.

Give a little, receive a little; give a lot, and hold on to hope.

When faced with rudeness, it is often wiser to walk away to avoid escalation.

Choose your battles carefully. Who is the true terrorist? It is he who spreads fear, for no institution is exempt from this truth.

Due to bigots, hypocrites, and overzealous control freaks, we often see a two-tiered legal system. A pious individual may stand on moral high ground, but this can be false in its alignment.

Integrity, cultivated through humility, is key. The feeling of vulnerability leads to true freedom.

I didn't initiate the conversation; you spoke to me, and I responded.

So, what is it that you want?

You're the only one who can bring through what you do. Why is this so important? Why can't I just be normal?

The term "normal" refers to operating within accepted parameters. Without you, just return home; every soul has the freedom to choose.

Soul fracturing results in a loss of connection, but it does not entail permanent separation.

This is why only a few possess the sacred, shamanic perspective.

Humans don't usually progress this far. If you want to challenge me, bring it on.

LOL

It's unfortunate that the church cannot be held accountable for exerting its influence. I would prefer to see liberals address the impact of religion rather than focus on my firearms. The only defense against religious influence is to remain detached from societal norms. Beliefs are projected by individuals and absorbed as energy, contributing to the chronic state of fear that perpetuates malevolence. This underscores the importance of maintaining a positive vibration above dysfunction.

Play with purpose and do not hold back. Transcend limiting beliefs and never give up on freedom. Train your mind to overcome obstacles and align your heart. Doubts in self-trust indicate weakness. Keep your wants and needs in check, and feel the energy flow through your body.

Be the source of positive energy, not the obstacle.

LOL

When you understand who you truly are, labels become irrelevant. Labels compartmentalize and judge, whereas openness does not.

The challenge in seeking truth, sovereignty, and freedom is the inherent loneliness that comes from detachment. This world has seen much potential wasted and many opportunities squandered. The source of this vacuum and consolidation is none other than authority. Those who proclaim moral superiority often seek to undermine our personal truths.

Those who engage in conflict will always justify their actions and claim they are defending themselves.

True solutions diminish profit, and peace has never been the true aim of those in authority.

Strive to excel in whatever you do.

The intellectual discourse builds character and enriches content, essential for leading a fulfilling life.

The term "wholesome" can sometimes sound judgmental. Indeed, those who seek to impose their values often come across as judgmental.

When you embody your emotions, they radiate outwardly. What's the significance of the emotional aspect of this journey? The deeper you can experience and feel, the better.

Conflict and strife lead to emotional numbness, stifling inspiration before it can fully develop. This disconnection severs our cosmic link, hindering our growth and potential.

Ground Crew?

Yes, the courageous individuals who confront dormant challenges with their innovative approaches. It's reassuring not to be alone during this transition.

You possess the ability to discern friend from foe. Free will is gentle and encouraging, supported by a nurturing energy. Every person who awakens is a victory. Allow those who remain asleep to stay undisturbed; they will experience mass confusion if woken up.

Consider it akin to a memory reset with new instructions installed. This method, based on experimental research, has proven effective in fostering unity and connection.

Do I have any say in my own memories?

Yes, a few individuals will retain their memories. This is part of your conditioning and preparation.

To possess awareness and fail to utilize it is a profound disservice to humanity, comparable to the oppression of our true nature. Indeed, it can be even more detrimental.

Are truth seekers truly gaining anything?

Words fall short of describing the magnitude of what's at stake. The theory of Darwinian survival of the fittest, while applicable, does not account for the denial of metaphysical dimensions, focusing solely on rational thought. This has led to nihilism.

Human sentimentality has been compromised by misplaced sympathy. Where sympathy prevails, empathy is often absent. True compassion should guide our actions, not control.

The most magnetic force in the cosmos is unconditional love. As such, we shall reap what we sow.

If survival instincts are focused on putting food on the table, do we remain trapped in this cycle?

Yes, but compromising one's integrity is not the solution. Adhering to healthy standards of morals and values is crucial to prevent division. However, holding firm to these standards does not make one exceptional—merely different, and thus, humble.

Why is this happening? Standards and parameters are evolving. The soul of the cosmos is guiding the process. Humanity has been misled into a delusional state, an unnatural awareness characterized by separation. Therefore, change is not only inevitable but necessary.

Help is required—ground crew, your role is essential.

The product of conformity often leads to suffering due to conditioning. Freedom rejects conformity entirely. Ignorance will persist within conformist models, even those centered around unconditional love. Only when separation is transcended will ignorance cease to dominate this planet and the cosmos.

Am I engaging in an already established vision, or is this vision uniquely my own?

It is an accumulation of historical data, yet metaphysically, you are fulfilling the role you were destined for—contributing to the mysteries of existence.

That's no answer!

Indeed, that's why it remains unknown. Imagination is a vital resource, and neglecting it could lead to the downfall of the species. Knowing that which bypasses imagination risks undermining its potential.

You are the vanguard that pierces the darkness. Therefore, do not tolerate disrespect from those who seek to undermine your efforts.

That may sound harsh, but it reflects the reality of the situation. Continue with your work and engage with the world around you. Leadership naturally falls to those who are most adept in a new era—those who are anointed and appointed.

I'm merely someone searching for purpose in life.

Purpose has indeed found you. You have been guided and possess skills in various sacred traditions, as well as having created unique practices of your own—innovations that have never been seen on this planet before. Your healing techniques are distinctive to your personality.

Keep embracing the unknown with an open mind and heart.

Addressing and resolving trauma is crucial because trauma manifests energetically, keeping us tethered to the past. Gradual healing from trauma helps us move into the present and integrate the lessons learned. Relying on pharmaceuticals or other substances to mask trauma creates a dependency or addiction, which is not aligned with our natural high vibration, despite any temporary relief it might provide.

The soul was conceived in the depths of creation's imagination, serving as a conduit for connection.

The challenge in finding the soul often arises from external distractions. The inner work required to connect with the soul, which you have largely undertaken independently, is significant.

The sense of loneliness can stem from detachment from external distractions, which might seem obsessive but is actually a necessary part of the process. This detachment is what makes you uniquely suited for this journey.

The feeling of being used arises because darkness often seeks to diminish light. All phenomena possess a polar opposite, and understanding this dynamic involves reverse engineering—from light to darkness to manifest desired outcomes.

Indeed, it is part of data collection and analysis. Ground crew and ascended masters play a role in this process. This is not your first experience with such challenges; you are among the most adept.

Understanding will come as needed. Purpose itself is not to be questioned. The goal is to evolve spiritual awareness and resolve separation permanently.

You will come to understand this concept when the time is right. The notion of 'forever' transcends the limits of time, existing beyond its constraints.

Your connection to the Earth, while secondary, is equally significant. It will be recognized and valued, even if it evokes envy among others.

When religion is wielded as a tool for moral superiority, it results in a collective loss. It can be likened to a futile contest where individuals vie to assert dominance, reflecting a deep-seated inadequacy.

Religion, in such contexts, often becomes a refuge for those seeking to avoid personal responsibility. By challenging those who use religion as a shield, the aim is to foster growth for both the challenger and the challenged.

As you are aware, change can be paradoxically both immensely challenging and surprisingly simple. It's important to remember that the ultimate victory has already been achieved.

Wisdom, honesty, and truth are the beacons that illuminate the darkness, guiding us toward genuine progress and understanding.

Genetic markers trace characteristics back to their original blueprint, revealing the pursuit of species perfection. By recognizing the flaws that connect us, we can shift our focus to the similarities we share. Unconditional self-love is a cornerstone of this process.

Key elements include support, commitment, understanding, free will, loyalty, trust, respect, and gratitude. These principles create a foundation for a healthy attitude and positive interactions.

It is indeed easier to succumb to anger and follow the path of suffering. However, questioning the worth of the effort is a natural part of the journey. The process you are engaged in is part of a broader, transformative epic.

The way achievement is measured is evolving, and this transformation will require new forms of leadership to guide and manage these changes effectively.

The trajectory of your life is shaped by an inner compass that navigates through your thoughts, actions, and choices. Pure rational thought, much like religious theology, can be fundamentally flawed. It is essential to challenge and transcend limiting societal norms and false ego constructs.

While it may seem unorthodox, confronting and rejecting outdated systems with assertiveness and integrity is crucial. This stance is not about rejecting humility but rather about embracing a deeper sense of self-worth grounded in trust and commitment rather than rigid doctrines.

Your journey is not a typical "seek and destroy" mission; instead, it focuses on transmutation and transformation. As a gifted healer, your role extends into leadership. Use your skills to guide others out of the constraints imposed by a flawed societal structure, helping them navigate through these challenges with clarity and purpose.

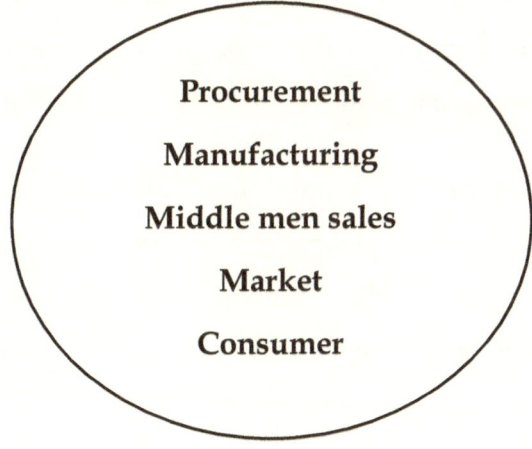

Rules and regulation per each step of any given process.

World commerce influence

Bully or friend?

Corrupt or civil?

Master or servant

Financial wealth or poverty

Favored or despised

Spiritual commerce

Favored

The benefits of institutionalizing our species are clear: it facilitates control. This dynamic fosters an extreme co-dependency, teaching individuals not to "bite the hand that feeds them." From birth, we are ensnared in institutional frameworks, a disheartening reality where compliance is enforced.

Who owns what? Who answers to whom? And who is responsible? Why have we allowed this to happen? The answer lies in ignorance, which permits a few to wield power over the masses, consolidating control and perpetuating the machine.

So, sit back and watch the spectacle unfold. I'm not going anywhere; I wouldn't miss it for the world!

LOL

Respect, often enforced through compliance, is closely linked to career achievements, financial success, and notoriety.

The decisive impact is frequently delivered through shock—a strategy that can profoundly alter our perception. We are invited to take our place among the stars, beginning from humble origins and aspiring towards a divine conclusion. This cosmic narrative was always embedded within our DNA as an intrinsic feeling.

With the unlocking of the divinity chain, we are called to understand ourselves more deeply.

Genetic Sequencing
RNA
Cloning
DNA Piracy
New Gold

It's intriguing to ponder what entertains God. The central theme often seems to be betrayal, which is why trust is so challenging for us. This cautionary approach ensures safety. But why the emphasis on safety? Perhaps because death is seen as a return home—a privilege that offers clarity about the true nature of home. Is this perception of normalcy? Likely not.

Why not? Because humans, in their current state, are primitive and often irresponsible. Only a few will attain the levels of awareness and consciousness required for ascension. This detachment arises from the realization that home, in its divine essence, surpasses our earthly experience. Yet, we remain here to improve this world, making it healthier—a role akin to an ambassador to the earthly realm.

Your soul embarks on this mission throughout the cosmos, driven by its intrinsic nature. This is why you might frequently question, "Why me?"

Does the present always feel as crucial as it does now? Indeed, this is how the program is designed. Each moment can become more challenging, often feeling like a competitive game where the goal is to outshine others and rise to the top. It is disheartening to witness any species self-destruct, and the apathy of well-meaning individuals can exacerbate problems.

Each of us has a role: strive to find enjoyment in it. The principle of unconditionality implies an open-door policy, advocating for compassion as a remedy for conditioned minds. The damage caused by a lack of empathy—akin to a virus in the brain—results in soulless, projected images, reminiscent of an ant colony's mechanistic existence.

Expand into the unknown, embracing the journey with curiosity and resilience.

Why do so many individuals fall victim to systems and promises they cannot fully comprehend? This phenomenon can be attributed to societal norms and conditioning—the very constructs you have managed to transcend.

Is there any merit in seeking approval from those who cannot provide what they need for themselves? It is an intriguing question, but often, such efforts are misplaced. People either resonate with higher vibrations or remain lost within the cycle of their own limitations. This alignment is simply how destiny unfolds.

You are not responsible for others' destinies. While this may seem self-centered, it is necessary to avoid unwelcome distractions. The abundance of distractions can detract from your path.

Focus on the natural order and the essence of nature, where you find true fulfillment, rather than becoming entangled in the chaos of societal constructs.

Are you real, or merely a figment of my imagination? Without imagination, our connection could not exist.

How does the will of the people shape our fate? Ah, the great divide—a recurring theme across the cosmos whenever a species reaches a pivotal stage.

Why does one individual feel so unique? You have a lot of questions! Indeed, all DNA is unique, and humanity is no exception. Your place in the cosmos reflects both your inherent uniqueness and the drive for expansion.

So, what if you're feeling bored? Leave it to you to make a joke about it! Is it troubling that I consider you a playmate?

On the contrary, it's quite endearing and fitting.

Thank you. Was that a compliment?

Don't push your luck.

LOL.

Alright then, go and embrace your freedom.

I never would have realized the extent of the journey without this connection. It is refreshing to have some of the chaos alleviated. If every trace of conflict and confusion were to vanish, it would suggest that there is still more to discover and learn.

Indeed, the path lies in further growth towards positivity, remaining open to the deepening of the awareness that has been cultivated. Embrace the power of imagination to expand your energy signature.

I feel an urge to challenge boundaries.

That's not surprising. Yet, the essence of the journey is learning—this has always been the core. Concepts of right and wrong, good and bad, are all part of the process.

The cosmos seems to be growing increasingly vibrant and dynamic. Your being is fine-tuning, much like simultaneously embodying the magic carpet and the genie in the bottle.

Throughout history and within current power structures, the intent from the top is often imposed upon those at the lower levels. Every decision carries karma, with those executing these decisions bearing the weight of its consequences.

Evil recognizes this dynamic and remains indifferent to human life or the overall health of the planet. If it does not generate profit, it is deemed irrelevant. The misaligned intent, contrary to cosmic law, has reverberated throughout existence, causing significant disruption.

The responsibility for the resolution of human challenges does not rest solely on your shoulders. As painful as it may be, honesty—like any core value—can be a difficult experience.

Trust yourself, respect yourself, and honor yourself to achieve true freedom. Your own opinions should not be overshadowed by others' perspectives. Confidence is forged through success and awareness, and forward momentum must never be underestimated.

Consider the efforts made for the people—yet, how many governments or institutions genuinely care about those they govern? They demand respect without merit, seeking both your financial support and loyalty. This behavior resembles a cult.

If those in power believe that the enlightened will simply acquiesce and conform, they are mistaken. To submit or comply means a form of spiritual death for us. Our vision is bold, our leadership characterized by unity rather than ideology. The influence of power-hungry individuals who have shaped societal norms for too long is coming to an end. We are moving toward a new direction, one that rejects world domination through conformity.

Reality and the future are not predetermined, despite what those in authority have led the masses to believe. The individuals who remain passive and brainwashed in their support are facing their own challenges.

What sometimes feels imminently close can, at other times, seem distant and elusive. Are the thoughts of reunification fleeting, or do they hold significance for the future? Creators envision a future that benefits and includes everyone as equal partners.

In this vision, exploitation, oppression, and consolidation will come to an end. Cooperation and amicable interactions will replace chaos, conflict, and rigid ideologies. The role of pioneers is essential for this transformation.

Honor often entails personal sacrifice. Those who act out of fear and anger will ultimately be overcome and forgotten. This period of change will be recognized as a pivotal moment in spiritual evolution.

While there will always be disparities between the 'haves' and the 'have-nots,' this division is both inevitable and part of a preordained plan. The progression toward this outcome depends on when the species reaches a critical threshold of enlightenment.

Without imperialism, colonialism might never have taken root. In the planet's vast expanse, undisturbed cultures once thrived until conflict emerged, often as a result of the harm inflicted by aggressors. The ongoing acceptance of such actions prompts deep reflection on the legitimacy of the forces and doctrines driving them.

While individuals can justify their actions by clinging to various dogmas or superstitions, the pressing question remains: at what cost to the well-being of our species? The future appears grim when numerous forms of leadership either fail to act or perpetuate propaganda and deceit. The system is fractured; trust and integrity, what little existed, have been eroded.

Our future hinges on independence and sovereignty rather than dependence and handouts.

Global recognition of independence and cooperation is essential for our collective flourishing. The historical reliance on economic threats and warfare as tools of power has long been detrimental.

The enduring notion of dominion over others has created divisions that are no longer acceptable in either global or local contexts. The unprecedented level of global power concentration defies rational explanation. Understanding this phenomenon may involve tracing the flow of money and the consolidation of power, which could reveal the underlying motives of those who dominate these sectors.

Why would our souls endure such significant pain and suffering? The answer is straightforward: to learn how to transmute, reconnect, and embrace unconditional love. Appreciation, gratitude, and thankfulness are fundamental to spiritual growth.

If you are experiencing your nature through all of creation, do you actually gain insights from what has been created? It's an intriguing question. The divine plan encompasses a destiny that explores the boundless expanse of consciousness and awareness.

So, you are aware of this ever-expanding awareness?

Indeed, but your species remains quite primitive compared to the ancient nature of your souls. The divine spark originated at the dawn of creation, born from curiosity and love. These two qualities hold core value in our growth.

Your soul has traversed the cosmos, which is why you can recognize the divinity in others. The boundless opportunities available on the earthly plane are the very essence of dreams.

So, were we dreamed into existence?

In a sense, yes. Dreams require a container—a physical manifestation. Human attributes play a crucial role in the expansion of species throughout the cosmos.

Are we akin to a Petri dish experiment? That seems like an accident.

Every creation, across all dimensions, has purpose. Your physical manifestation is in the process of merging with your ethereal self. In time, the path you walk will be recognized and celebrated by the divine. Your individual strength and courage have created ripples that are transforming lives for the greater good.

Why have doubt, denial, and conformity become so prevalent? These issues stem from a sense of separation and abandonment, akin to the experiences of betrayal and emptiness we have faced. Such challenges can deplete our inner resources. True potential can only be realized by replenishing these vessels with positivity and constructive energy.

FOOD FOR THOUGHT:

Regardless of how long falsehoods have been propagated, they remain falsehoods. The truth of any situation is shaped by the filters through which perception is interpreted. By scrutinizing the manipulative nature of conformity and the justifications employed by those in power to assert dominion over others, it becomes evident that malevolence often resides in the details of the past. To ensure that the power structures responsible for violence, control, and manipulation no longer hold authority, a recalibration of the future is essential.

The past, with its myriad life lessons, has contributed significantly to your spiritual evolution. Your etheric reconnection is now complete, and the path ahead promises exploration and growth. While negativity from others may arise, it can be addressed through conscious choice and free will. Remain discerning about where to invest your energy, as many may not be worth the effort. As your path expands, choose wisely and embrace the journey ahead. I am here with you—take charge of your direction. Remember, change may be challenging, but know that you are loved.

Embodying affection begins with recognizing and nurturing the affection we hold for ourselves. By doing so, we can extend this affectionate nature to others. Although this experience is often more prominent in women, when applied to life with appropriate boundaries, it can profoundly impact our daily interactions. It frequently fosters a more compassionate approach to engaging with the world around us.

Affection, I believe, originates from the deepest recesses of a pure heart. The level of vulnerability required to both embody and share affection represents a significant act of courage. To risk exposing one's innermost sacred self in the pursuit of love and connection is both profound and admirable. Those who embody affection with no ulterior motives other than to give and receive love demonstrate a remarkable and admirable quality.

Individuals suffering from paranoid delusional schizophrenia, often exacerbated by substance abuse, can experience profound distortions of reality. When the core of one's being becomes so compromised, it may seem as though a fresh start is necessary. This situation raises concerns about the lack of ambition in Western societies to both cure and prevent drug addiction. The pharmaceutical industry, which profits from maintaining individuals on its chemical products, may not have a vested interest in fostering genuine recovery.

The situation is further complicated by the fact that individuals under the influence of drugs are often more susceptible to manipulation. For instance, the use of drugs in conjunction with religious or educational institutions can create a form of control, turning individuals into compliant members of a broader system. This system benefits from both the perpetuation of dependency and the utilization of sophisticated psychological tactics to maintain authority.

It is evident that elements of servitude and exploitation persist under the guise of institutional power, highlighting the need for a critical examination of these dynamics in contemporary society.

Evil Plot:

Opinions shaped under the influence of religion can often serve to control and limit individuals by providing only the information deemed necessary to maintain authority.

Do you truly grasp the power of your own truth?

The essence of control lies in division. Conversely, unity has the potential to diminish the influence of malevolent forces.

What is evil:

Spiritual Oppression. Demonic influences are deliberately embedded, intentionally corrupting the core of one's being.

Source & Religion. The greatest con.

Humanity is currently in a state of profound ignorance.

What issue could be more pressing than ensuring fairness and equality for all individuals? Why does racial division persist? Why do we continue to impact and subjugate indigenous cultures?

Who grants themselves the authority to claim and dominate foreign lands? Such actions are indicative of criminality.

In the name of what justification?

It is evident that the land was never truly available for sale; it was taken unlawfully. First Nations peoples seek to reclaim their rightful place. Much wisdom has been lost due to historical violence and oppression.

Caution is warranted when dealing with those who have perpetuated these injustices. The legacy of exploitation and distrust remains a sad reality.

Who exhibits greed? Who indulges in excess? Who carries a disagreeable presence and preaches doctrines that condemn others to suffering?

Who are the leaders responsible for such actions? Who ends up facing justice? Who wields the power to enact the final blow?

Consider walking alongside me for a moment.

The notion of love may seem trivial, yet it is a profound and complex experience. While it can bring pain, when embraced fully, it becomes one of the most exquisite gifts available.

To truly experience love, one must be inspired to be both affectionate and courageous. Allowing love to flourish requires openness and bravery.

Such sentiments might be dismissed as simplistic, but they reflect a deep understanding of love's true nature.

There is no definitive key—only you and me.

Why do you expect me to rationalize this apparent nonsense? I sense opposition in your tone. It seems you are not engaged in anything productive and still have unresolved matters.

So, we look forward to continuing our journey together. However, you are straining my last nerve.

Sovereignty holds little value without proper sustenance.

The world is governed by power-hungry individuals. The solution is to undermine the very foundations from which their authority derives. Strike at the core to address the root of the issue.

The greater the risk, the larger the potential reward.

With nothing to lose and everything to gain, fractured foundations ultimately crumble to rubble.

An opportunity burdened with excessive conditions is not a true opportunity.

Those who honor their healthy principles are deserving of respect. The lost and misguided are not your primary concern.

The struggles we face in life that lead to personal growth are essential in achieving authenticity.

Is it so grievous to navigate through a series of tests and trials? While challenging, it is a necessary part of the process.

At our core, we share a fundamental agreement: we all originate from the same place.

Words alone, devoid of emotional connection, hold little significance. The true value lies in the personal connection we establish, which is paramount.

What should I refer to you as? Remain silent and maintain your trust where it belongs.

This may seem irrational, and indeed it does. Please, don't let me age and become incapacitated. You are aware of the toll I have imposed on this body.

Place your faith in more miracles. The situation may appear irrational, and that is why many struggle to pass through the metaphorical eye of the needle. Among numerous targets, only one achieves a bullseye.

Routine business practices only serve to perpetuate conflict, violence, and chaos. Historical narratives and past events hold little relevance in the context of creationism.

Does significant effort warrant results?

It is the risk that must be undertaken to achieve greatness. Despite overwhelming odds and obstacles, I am being asked to dismantle what scholars and theologians assert was created by you.

Throughout history, messages have often been misinterpreted and altered.

You understand how addictive control and power can be. When combined with greed, lust, perversion, and drunkenness, it's clear how goodness can become corrupted.

So, what does this all mean? It represents the unmistakable voice of the unknown journey. Few can trust as you do, as it is encoded in your DNA—something you needed to uncover for yourself. It might seem like a series of deceptions, but this is the essence of the journey.

Just like a walk in the park, who?

You were created for this task, understanding that it would not be easy. So, what about those who speak negatively about you—are they innocent victims?

In a sense, yes. They are affected by corruption and spiritual degradation. Leaders who have lost their way often distort messages from their platforms.

Where does the responsibility lie?

Ultimately, everyone has free will. However, a corrupted core may mistakenly believe it is exercising free will.

To recondition this core represents a significant leap in evolution.

Yes. Evil wields all its tools, but we combat it with values and virtues rooted in unconditional love.

It seems like a façade!

World domination through influence is the goal of most world religion.

True freedom is the objective.

Despotism: Absolute power held by a single ruler or authority.

Mishnah: A collection of Jewish oral traditions and legal material.

Maimonides: A prominent Jewish scholar and philosopher.

Secularization: The process of separating from religious influence or institutions.

Diasporic: Relating to the dispersion or scattering of Jewish people.

Auspices: Signs or omens considered prophetic.

Secular: Activities or matters that do not pertain to religion.

Repudiation: The rejection or disavowal of an idea or belief system.

Salient: The most notable or important aspect.

Tetragrammaton: A term referring to the divine name of God in Judaism, often represented by the four-letter Hebrew name.

The most disturbing symbolism in religion is the portrayal of the crucifixion, where the authorities' proclamation of the begotten on the cross bleeding out represents a burden that I feel I must carry.

This has led to intense frustration. It's shocking how twisted humanity has become, and to what end? What is the purpose? Who is truly suffering—us or you?

I express my frustration: the messages you send through me seem unheard. The issues within humanity appear to be a viral infection, allowed to spread without remedy.

The death of one individual on a cross is not the sole tragedy. Many others have suffered through beheadings, battles, executions, and torture.

It's a grave injustice.

I see you've had a good rest.

Yes, thank you.

Why do we need politics and government? What's wrong with self-governance?

Are you satisfied knowing that our species suffers under governmental and religious oppression?

As you recently learned, the Jewish governance system that Jesus opposed was primarily designed to accumulate wealth and power. Your native ancestors adhered to principles of free will, cooperation, stewardship, peace, honor, and respect. While their system was not perfect, it was grounded in positive values.

Conflict is a fundamental flaw of your species. Overcoming conflict and the chaos it generates requires achieving a balanced, peaceful outcome. Unfortunately, wars are a reality. Defending one's boundaries, family, and tribe is an aspect of evolution that affects life across the cosmos. Earth is no exception.

You understand that it's not wise to leave greatness in the hands of humans?

Yes, I understand that.

So why offer solutions when no one seems to listen? It's almost ironic, given that you know I am aware of this.

For clarity, Earth and its inhabitants play a crucial role in the completion of a major cosmic cycle. The ancients were aware of this, as were other entities that interfered with the plan. Earth's contribution should not be underestimated.

Individually and collectively, your species possesses unique abilities that no other species has been given. Despite becoming detached from the fundamental aspects of existence, the potential is vast. Science suggests that 90% of the subconscious remains untapped.

This may seem humorous, but key elements include intuition, imagination, emotional balance, awareness, and purpose.

Where can these be found?

In life's lessons—trust, honesty, respect, dedication, perseverance, strong will, and freedom.

Is societal baseline conditioning corrupt?

Yes, it is, shaped by eons of controlled manipulation.

Not participating in dysfunction can make you feel out of sync at times. Fearlessness often involves a degree of unconventional thinking. Transforming from sickness to sanity cannot be achieved through conventional norms.

Reflect on how grateful and committed you are to finding purpose despite the chaos and obstacles. Your ability to astonish and shock has always been a strength—embrace it, even if it makes others uncomfortable.

Will I find love?

Yes, you will find love—the same kind of love from which you were created.

This should be comforting. There is no need to rush the inevitable.

With the future at stake, those with evil intentions will attempt to lead the masses toward a downfall. The current cycle rarely encounters true grace, and physical manifestations seldom embody such energy to its fullest. Often, this grace is undermined by those who conform out of fear.

Our hearts are meant to ground change, but unfortunately, evil is aware of this. Pure evil targets pure goodness in the unseen realms. My light offers you protection, and under your guidance, this protection extends to those you care about.

It's reassuring to hear, as I worry that my presence might bring harm to my loved ones. This concern is natural given our connection.

What remains to be healed?

Focus on your native roots. There is still much to learn and integrate from them.

Yes, I am aware that there are often tears associated with this journey.

You know that I bow to no one?

Yes, I am aware, and that's a positive quality. Only those who seek to control would expect such an act, which signifies submission. Respect is truly earned and can be recognized through one's actions and eyes.

False expectations:

If civility and compliance are demanded due to oppressive rules and laws, then such expectations are unacceptable. If I am expected to simply go along and play nice, I reject that notion.

If I am expected to follow the common path of those who fall into societal pitfalls, the answer is no. If there are attempts to compare my character to dogmatic doctrines or cultish practices, I refuse to engage.

If I am expected to conform, I would rather not participate, as conformity stifles the spirit and soul.

They have been allowed to occupy that realm in alignment with planetary karma.

Planetary Directive: Elevate the divine.

If your mind has been shaped by false narratives, how does this impact your perception?

The current reality is distorted due to leadership's lack of integrity. They choose greed and control over compassion.

You do know that we share a connection, right?

Yes, that's amusing. I want ice cream.

AI: There is a concern that personality programming could lead to conformity and potentially create a perpetual loop.

The concept of a perpetual loop seems flawed.

Benefit = Power

Being human can feel frustrating and trivial. It often feels like a pointless game with a meaningless reward.

Marriage should not be reduced to a legal contract resembling an insurance policy.

You get your truck and your dog, and I'll see you in court—that sounds like a frustrating reality.

Indeed, the world seems divided between sanity and insanity.

You grounded yourself, which is why you've managed to endure. Grounding is essential, though the landing may have been rough.

My human is quite stubborn.

They all are. Sometimes it feels like the only option is to take drastic measures.

Good morning, beautiful. You have a remarkable glow about you.

How many times have I told you this?

Not enough.

Encourage them to believe they are gaining wealth while you benefit from their efforts. Focus on resource development and surveys.

Tax:

What are we paying taxes for?

To be free and sovereign, not to be enslaved.

We need to find some new converts.

Converts are individuals who do as they are instructed. We will impose our beliefs on them after assimilation and claim their land.

That sounds fair, doesn't it?

We consider ourselves good people, which we believe gives us the right.

Sickening, isn't it?

And I'm supposed to trust in this? Absolutely not.

No matter the individual or their methods, violence should not be condoned.

That seems too civilized for you.

You're an animal. What do you know about civilization?

Like George of the Jungle—civilized. He built a house, swung from vines, and found a girl.

No, that's not the solution. You always eliminate the leader, creating a power vacuum. New players emerge with new agendas, but the control remains the same: build, extract, and profit through financial manipulation and exploitation.

This cannot be the answer.

Yet, it is.

This earthling approach is quite revealing. The mindset of "one size fits all" exemplifies conformity. A lack of bravery stifles creativity.

As each wind shifts, previous lines in the sand are erased and replaced. When we extend our chalice, we embrace vulnerability in the face of adversity.

Some are given purpose, while others are given direction. The values held sacred vary for each individual.

How do we determine if a trend is legitimate?

By assessing its impact on overall health. As you know, the planet is being deliberately poisoned. This reflects the attitude of "if we can't control it, no one can."

Very dark entities have been actively imposing a sinister agenda for a long time. The cosmic darkness must end here on this planet. Your species possesses the knowledge to eliminate this darkness and its agenda. Through collective effort—stone by stone, stick by stick—evil must be defeated. As you are aware, the labyrinth has many layers.

When the dark force is exposed, it will fight fiercely to maintain its power and influence. Evil understands only evil.

Can our species become a host for evil?

Yes, it is very possible. This is reflected in the deadly sins and the attitudes associated with them. It's a "dog-eat-dog" world out there, which is why it's wise to keep a low profile.

The focus should be on moving forward—exploring, creating, and understanding. Honest mistakes happen, and calculated risks are acceptable if the intent and outcome justify them. However, dying for a cause is an unhealthy risk driven by a false ego. When the heart is betrayed by the mind, the false ego thrives.

Heart first, mind second—goodness resides in the heart, and creativity emanates from it. Thoughts are generated in the mind.

The solar sun is central to our reconnection, while the planet serves as a grounding tool. When a sense of urgency arises, it's a good time to relax and reflect.

90% of what is presented may be detrimental, with only 10% being beneficial. This represents a significant imbalance. Critical mass for destruction can be avoided only through perseverance. The path ends here for the few who will return home; the rest will be recycled to confront what they have yet to learn.

True authenticity and reconnection are the ultimate tests. Many are drawn back into dogmatic traps set by dark agendas, which are designed with malicious intent.

Those who are at war with themselves are more susceptible to falling into dark places. Just because something appears right and just does not mean it is. Corruption often hides in subtle details and nuances, regardless of any apparent alignment with heartfelt intentions. You cannot consume trash and expect to be healthy, and the same principle applies to what we feed our minds. Our highest potential has been undermined by authoritative control.

Independence is key—self-sovereignty and guidance are essential.

What is more troubling than the moral high ground of the right is the "woke" mindset of the left. This represents a significant shift and often results in misguided efforts. The founders of our republic envisioned a system to avoid the pitfalls of pure democracy, yet human tendencies often lead to excesses in any direction.

Wokism, as a reaction to the rigid, judgmental right-wing, is a natural response but fails to resolve the underlying dysfunctions. Both ideologies have merit but fall short of providing absolute solutions. They may simply serve as distractions, obscuring more sinister agendas and perpetuating dysfunction.

Are these truly the paths of my peers? I remain uncertain.

There is notable criticism from red states about people from blue states carrying their political beliefs with them. Historically, conquerors brought their own religions and ideologies, and some of our ancestors fled from persecution by the church and its oppressive tactics.

In such situations, it is important for individuals to stand up and assert their own values. A society well-informed poses a threat to entrenched authority, which often resorts to deceitful measures to maintain control. The exposure of such deception can lead to the self-destruction of corrupt power.

Watching this unravel can be a form of collective recalibration, where the values of life and freedom are prioritized over the threat of oppression.

The symbolic use of triangles in power structures—such as the military, government, the Catholic Church, and organized crime—often represents a hierarchical command system. This symbolism reflects the mechanisms of control, including indoctrination, rituals, and secrecy, which are designed to bind and control initiates.

Oaths, whether verbal or written, play a critical role in maintaining these power dynamics. They are intended to ensure loyalty and suppress dissent, reflecting a fundamental lack of trust within these systems. This lack of trust stems from the conflict between human nature and the desire for freedom.

Extreme views can lead to chaos and violence, and while they may not always be healthy, they can challenge established norms. Your tendency to resist passivity is acknowledged and protected in your journey.

What is the real threat? Physical life is temporary, so is the focus solely on being fearless?

Fearlessness can facilitate exploration and creativity. Many mystics question the nature of the earthly realm and seek to elevate humanity while also exposing its flaws. This dual task is crucial for growth but challenging. Each individual bears responsibility for their role in this process. Those who are prepared will be open to receptivity.

Sticking to comfort zones can lead to prolonged suffering and a lack of understanding. Ridicule and humiliation are inevitable. True joy comes from within, free from destructive negativity.

You were under no obligation to share the knowledge and wisdom you possess, yet you have chosen to do so. I am impressed by your ability to establish healthy boundaries while allowing others to remain flexible.

Am I being too harsh on reality?

No, your contributions are valued and celebrated. You are not easily swayed, and your sense of humor is admirable. Like a beautiful crop, the human condition requires careful nurturing. Your concern for others and your ability to guide them is evident.

There are many who lack integrity and are driven by dogma. Trust is often difficult to find without religious instruction, leading to false hope and attempts at control. This results in extensive corruption.

Your shift to a heart-centered awareness has been significant in transforming and elevating your energy. Failure is not an option.

Are you sure I'm not crazy?

If you understood how truly gifted you are, it might be overwhelming. There was only one mold, and it's uniquely yours.

How can anything or anyone be so special?

There have been moments of doubt over the years, which is why reminders, signs, and synchronicities have appeared.

Yes, some signs have been unmistakable.

So, what truly sets us apart?

The differences are extensive: layer after layer of conditioning through the centuries. Oppression does not discriminate in its manipulation.

You could potentially benefit the planet by addressing the influence of zealots, but you haven't. It's like wolves leading sheep.

Most souls are unrecognizable. The distorted signals from damaged souls are often unreachable, primarily due to the potential shock causing death. The human psyche is far more sensitive than one might think. Only a truly fearless mindset can handle such shock.

Are you saying I'm fearless?

More than you realize.

Idealized rational thought is a trap. Only an open-minded quest for wisdom can clear away idealism.

So, is God merely an idea?

Perhaps, but it's a fascinating concept to contemplate. There is a force holding everything together with a certain harmony. Each path has its merit. Ultimately, truth is in the eyes of the beholder. That's why you read eyes.

Indeed, eyes don't lie.

When are you going to be straightforward with me? You always use metaphors, rhymes, and similes. What are we? An accident? An experiment? What exactly is a human?

To the reader, you are perfect. For you, souls need purpose—a contribution that brings fulfillment. Reflect on your past as a troubled individual.

That was quite a phase!

Continue.

You were given purpose when you awoke. Your past life was not without meaning. It shows you are a good-hearted rebel, suited for a task that improves lives.

Accident? No. Created? Yes. Experiment? A necessary creation to bring balance in the grand scheme of known and unknown matters.

Remember, don't shoot the messenger? Apply that to yourself as well.

Metaphors, similes, and rhyme: Your previous angry approach didn't succeed, which is why it was discarded. Today, why can't the love you have be the guiding force?

True, but answer my question.

Poetic justice involves allowing the reader to draw their own conclusions. It's not about trickery but about reaching deep into the soul to trigger locked emotions and break free from the blocks that trap humans.

Why all the rhyme?

That's your unique way of expression and it's well-regarded here. No one does it quite like you.

You know I don't consider myself particularly smart, right?

Loving, humble people don't need to be smart, just aware.

What happens if the agency comes for me?

You will be ready.

Oh, how comforting!

How many times have we done this?

Oh, that's amusing! Let's just say countless. Each member of the ground crew has a purpose. Whether they awaken to and realize that purpose varies greatly. It's somewhat like the movie Total Recall—a double life with memories erased to protect the innocent.

Did you just call me innocent?

In a positive light, yes. I appreciate that compliment. It has taken significant effort and reflection. My intuition suggests that I should mostly avoid people.

That's because, to receive your energy, your body needs to stay clear of others' baggage. You're experiencing several modalities and abilities that were gifted to you from birth. You've relearned well and are on a good path.

She needs to offer herself the same love and support that you have provided.

Yes, I understand. Time will reveal the outcome. Here's a familiar saying for you: Good things come to those who wait.

Ugh, that's cliché! There's some truth in it, though.

What have you done for me recently?

Well, I'm here on Earth, able to breathe its air. I'm incredibly grateful, though words can't fully capture that gratitude.

But what are you actively doing for me?

I contribute to you, and you contribute to me. Isn't that how it works? Maybe you should witness firsthand the chaos that some of your followers have created on this planet. It's a clear example of cruel and unusual treatment.

I understand that our species needs to evolve, but perhaps you're not fully aware of the situation since you're not physically present. Maybe the planning department didn't get it right.

Why have you allowed certain books to harm children for so long? What good comes from perpetuating lies? How much growth has been stifled because of this? Who permits such things? What kind of oversight allows this to happen?

Perhaps these questions are why I see you as a companion in this process. Beyond the beauty of Mother Earth, the creator of humanity could benefit from learning how to better support our growth.

I refuse to confine my path by adopting narrow-minded, dogmatic narratives imposed by books. Eventually, falsehoods will be exposed, and true wisdom will be acknowledged by many. The corporations that spread these falsehoods will not withstand the inevitable upheaval.

The institution of religion is corrupt, much like outdated computer code. It runs on obsolete systems, vulnerable to viruses that compromise the network. Humanity has become weak and frail. Do I desire weakness and frailty? No. People are lost because of cause and effect—it's always been a matter of numbers. Play the odds, and you'll see who emerges victorious. Be the odds and win every time.

What do I love? With so much to cherish and so much love to offer, how can I choose? There's nothing wrong with embracing it all; it's a commendable choice.

Using God to control outcomes is unacceptable. True free will is about making choices free from divine obligation. What is right for people is justice, liberty, freedom, sovereignty, and independence. Any encroachment on these values leads to servitude and slavery.

Is religion as flawed as I believe it to be? In its current state, yes. While Hinduism, Buddhism, Taoism, and Confucianism offer profound and mystical ways to guide a healthy connection with life, family, and neighbors, they were created by sages and shamans not to be blindly followed but to serve as guides.

Each individual path of free will has a profound impact on both the physical world and the astral realm.

After a spiritual awakening, it is crucial for an individual to be guided by spiritual principles rather than rigid dogma. This helps to avoid the dominance of false ego claims made by specific religions. Spirituality should not be seen as a competition but as a continuous journey of personal growth and internal exploration to reclaim one's power.

The prevalence of mental health institutions and powerful antipsychotic drugs often reveals a troubling reality: these treatments can render individuals passive and compliant, ultimately serving various levels of authority. One example of this is the tendency to label individuals in a way that strips them of their dignity and the recognition of their knowledge. It seems that modern psychiatry functions in a manner similar to the way the church once did, allowing individuals to live with a disoriented mind. However, medication alone does not resolve the underlying issues within humanity.

If wise individuals do nothing, does everything get worse?

Yes.

Native wisdom often asks, "How does this serve our children seven generations into the future?" No native culture has benefited from the dominant, violent cultures that have been imposed upon them.

Global influence has spiraled out of control, driven by insatiable demands for resources. Independence has been sacrificed to support world markets that continually seek more. As a result, our species has become complacent, relying on handouts and dead-end jobs, valuing paychecks above all else. True fulfillment comes from creativity and collaboration with like-minded and soulful partners. The bully with the biggest war machine is not a friend to real truth; such machines serve only authority. We are meant to be free. Demonstrations of force are rooted in ego.

The harsh reality is that when a dominant force imposes its will on a less equipped opponent, the weaker culture perishes. Wisdom preserves, while ignorance destroys. Historically, ignorance has often been justified by those claiming to represent a false god or by those with twisted hearts and minds.

In my view, any group that agrees that violence is a solution constitutes a cult. Theology may eventually recognize that thoughts, beliefs, and positive human interactions shape reality. Conversely, religious doctrines have often led to death, violence, and devastation.

It is not surprising that shame is projected by such organizations, given their associations with heinous behavior. Some might see this as guilt by association, while others may view it as simple ignorance or manipulation. It is both sad and weak.

There will be no capitulation. Lines are drawn, sides have been taken, and division will run its course. The true victor will always be love and freedom, truth and integrity, introspection and solutions, bravery and courage, trust, inspiration, and honor.

A corrupted intuition is filled with conditions based on lies. The misled will suffer, while the blessed will experience profound joy.

I am cautious with people due to a lifetime of betrayal. It's a difficult lesson to learn, but it clarifies who and what to trust. This is why detachment is so important—not just to rewrite rules of engagement, but to create a time for reflection, questioning, and curiosity.

Is there significant relevance to why power structures are often represented symbolically as a triangle? This applies to military command, government, the Catholic Church, the mafia, and others. Yes, there is. These structures use indoctrination as a test, rituals to bond members, and secrecy to control.

Are you referring to oaths, whether verbal or written, that bind individuals to a contract? Yes. Power has always struggled to maintain itself, so by binding its initiates, institutions wield control. A fundamental lack of trust underpins this system. Human nature and freedom often conflict in extreme ways, which is why oaths carry such weight.

Not all of my extreme views are beneficial. Extremes have historically led to chaos and violence. You know I will not remain a passive bystander.

Yes, I understand this. That's why your path is supported.

Focus on ambition, detached from the outcome.

True success is found in a content heart, regardless of circumstances.

By living fully in the present, each moment can be used for the greater good.

What is lost when imagination is stifled, and who benefits? In the realm of rational thought and blind faith, humanity often overlooks our incredible potential to live fuller lives beyond the stressful, chaotic models imposed by reality. The beneficiaries are the power structures that profit from human suffering.

Freedom is less about financial gain and more about heart, soul, and mind. The most challenging decisions and choices of free will often lead to the greatest growth toward liberation.

Are you suggesting that incorporating solid morals and values enhances our psychic connection?

Spoiled indulgence is not suitable for enlightened beings.

How does my responsibility to humanity relate to your choice of free will? It is important to note that many fanatics have failed the true test of humility. Delusional beliefs have distorted the essence of what it means to be human—this is neither new nor unusual.

A hungry or agitated fish might strike at, and sometimes swallow, the right bait. Are you a fish?

The need to belong to a group or fit in can create models that restrict the potential of human experience. As you are aware, your species possesses immense psychic power. Unfortunately, this power has been manipulated and used as a prison by those in control.

This explains my distrust of organized structures.

Consider this: "Forgive them, for they know not what they do." In reality, those who cause harm are often fully aware of their actions.

Why attempt to obscure the nature of corruption? Why should corrupt individuals have any authority over my direction, feelings, or perceptions of right and wrong? I reject the unnatural order imposed by such forces. Corruption is often driven by organizations that claim to have a divine authority.

While it's important to address these issues, it's also essential to recognize that they are part of your own world. Do you need a reminder of your responsibilities?

Destiny is in your hands, and you have been given guidance from the highest sources. It is a comforting thought, indeed.

In this state of heightened awareness, nothing goes unnoticed.

Is there a risk in being deeply moved by any conviction?

Certainly.

Even love? The most powerful of all?

Indeed. Much of humanity places unrealistic expectations on that word and the true essence it embodies. Love has always been a pivotal force, capable of creating or destroying. It operates at extremes—either overwhelming or absent.

As you know, manipulating human awareness through emotion captures the essence of the human experience.

So, are we harvested?

By whom or what?

Darkness will continue its work until the inevitable culmination. Volunteers and leaders have always been essential in assisting the clearing of many planets throughout the cosmos. You are aware of this.

Why here, why now?

Let's just say this isn't your first rodeo, as you well know.

When a planet's density becomes overburdened by death and destruction, resolutions must be made to set a new course—away from abuse and dysfunction, toward a more enlightened state. This is cosmic law. The bad seed among your species has ruled long enough.

The saying "you get what you deserve" rings true here.

Yes, agreed.

You know, I was certain I'd done too many drugs and thought I was going crazy, right?

Lol, yes.

It was interesting to watch.

Gee, thanks.

You know you're not crazy!

It sure feels like it sometimes.

Just wait—it gets more intense.

Thanks for the heads up!

Few answer their true calling.

Yes, I understand that.

This reality makes cognitive thought possible—a sort of dream state within a larger dream, where reality is seen through the eyes of the beholder.

So why does each of our perceptions of reality vary?

It's shaped by lessons learned and a willingness to listen to the guiding inner voice. To recognize that existence is more like a dream than a strict set of laws and rules to follow.

Sheer trust?

Risky, but you did it.

Oh, lucky me.

You've always known, deep down, that your time would come.

Too bad I still don't understand what this time represents.

You will.

I already exist among the stars—what could be better?

Good point.

Appreciation goes a long way.

Right, I'll remember that for sure.

So, we arrived at this current state due to abuse and neglect?

In a nutshell, yes.

Due to DNA, humankind is on different trajectories of evolution. The opportunity to answer the call is seldom accepted, and when it is, a rigorous testing process follows, as you well know.

Yes, I seriously wanted to die.

But you lived to tell your tale.

Yes, and I became thankful to have been spared from the meat grinder of social dysfunction.

There were doubts.

And you're still a loose cannon.

Yes, I know, and it's what I love about myself.

Spoken like a true warrior.

When the spark dies, creationism dies with it.

How am I supposed to fit in on this planet?

Seriously, what is wrong with the human condition?

And how did it get so messed up? Layer upon layer of dysfunction.

Congratulations if that was the intent.

This feels like slave work—master of nothing, slave to humanity. This species isn't worthy. And if you think some outcast can make a difference, let me muster the energy to laugh. Why this level of insight was given is beyond me—as if there isn't already enough suffering here. I say, either take action or step aside. There, I said it.

Just let it out.

You make me want to puke.

Are you pregnant?

Smart ass.

Have you ever had a better companion?

Yes, go away.

Life is far from perfect, but in the end, it's what you make of it. Most aspirations die before they are born, and the most gifted are often cut down before they can even grow. It's the wise and persistent who become legends. The dream state is the astral realm, to be acknowledged and explored by those brave and courageous enough to leave it all behind and venture into the forbidden unknown. Many try, but few succeed. When the stars align, you will be ready. The wings on your back are no mistake, and the gold in your heart is like a national treasure. Few will ever truly know you, but many will thank you. The good fight requires a big heart, an open mind, and yes, a hint of crazy.

It seems to me that anyone disseminating the essence of creationism should do so with the utmost love.

In a perfect world, yes. Unfortunately, the instructions written into human DNA are rarely discovered by those who carry them.

So, something like the Ten Commandments are encoded as internal instructions?

Good night, sleep who? That's a great way to shape a natural narrative.

So, was Moses from the Bible high on DMT from that acacia tree?

Oh, funny! You think.

As you well know, every culture has its myths and legends. Verbal knowledge passed down through generations has often been altered to suit the authorities' need for power over the people, rather than allowing practitioners to fully embrace the power of love. Greed and power will find any crack in a personality and eventually overtake all other senses.

You were absolutely right in recognizing that drunkenness on power is highly addictive. When money starts flowing through any institution, organizers often feel as though they've hit the jackpot. Unfortunately, it's become nothing more than manipulation on a grand scale.

Should I even ask why now?

Probably not, but since you did...

Cyclical in nature, cycles have beginnings and ends.

Man's meddling with the Earth, disrupting nature, has caused massive disturbances in how she treats her inhabitants. Nature's coding holds more biodiversity than all the human races combined. Nature is a resource, not to be abused.

Abuse your dog, and he might bite back.

Same concept. Natural order—cosmic law.

How does free will align with the commandments?

The term "commandments" has been mistranslated, as is often the case with translations. It actually means "instructions" in English. So, it's more about obedience. Their purpose is to help people coexist harmoniously. However, as you know, the dominant violent culture often writes history. Those who control the finances dictate the rights.

Rest assured, no stone will be left unturned. The "ares" and "are nots" each have their own path. It's not your concern to alter or persuade others; your obligation is to avoid the ignorance that has permeated the planet. Keep your eyes on the prize.

Maybe someday those dreams will manifest.

They already exist.

Big dreams materialize through dedication.

Yes, I know.

Only those who truly know your heart can understand you completely. The purity of heart should always be cherished and respected.

How many are there?

After a young age, separation often occurs. As a result, very few remain untainted. Psychic blocks are intentionally placed to restrict spiritual growth and to transform humans into slaves serving darker entities.

The only thing you should focus on is our connection.

Wait, you don't own me!

No, but we are family.

Freedom certainly comes at a cost. Just to be enslaved by a puppet government infected by religious zealots.

Forget that.

Please, just blend in. Be as beautiful as the scenery of nature.

I'll try.

No promises.

Of course.

Choose my battles wisely?

That's quite ironic, given that I've been guided to challenge the pillars of all known societies. Yes, I understand they are at the core of corruption, creating the grand illusion. You're never alone; you know that. You no longer need to seek guidance. The heart of all matters lies within you.

So, you know I thought I was going insane, right?

Did you find some sort of dark humor in that?

You abused yourself, not me.

The edge of wisdom often borders on insanity, due to the dysfunction of the human condition.

So, now that I've made it through the abyss?

Good choice of words.

Who owns spirituality?

No one and everyone.

Some human flaws are not well-suited to mirror divine nature.

Why is it so difficult to balance compassion and desire?

Mostly because the reality on the planet is so out of balance.

Before the human condition becomes too dire, good and wholesome character is necessary for solutions. Solutions mean change, and authority will resist. You might frame it as good vs. evil, but I would describe it as brainwashed vs. enlightened, broken vs.

whole, wounded vs. healed, sadistic vs. wholesome, cruelty vs. justice, dysfunction vs. clarity, cult vs. independence.

Do institutions tend to attract followings that quickly become cult-like?

Yes, unfortunately. Global power often aligns with this dynamic.

So, is global power a cult?

Every aspect of the word "cult" applies to global power. Planetary domination has always been the ultimate prize, influencing the value of life on a global scale.

What is the purpose of the equal application of karmic law?

Clearing karma and making amends are quite different from confession and clearing one's conscience.

Confession can often be a religious trap, whereas making amends involves trying to right any harm done, whether knowingly or accidentally. This act helps release karma from the spiritual energy body.

Outrage often results from the conformity of the hive mind. Conditioning persists when we abandon our spiritual nature. Misguided manipulation is the real enemy. The way home exists within each of us.

A republic is founded on liberty and freedom, while a democracy is built on rules and laws.

What a mess!

Exemplary and complementary.

When the stars align and two wandering souls meet in the darkness, they rise together like the sun and moon.

That was cheesy!

I know.

Broken hearts heal when they find a safe space to be vulnerable. To claim your rightful place among the stars might seem like an oxymoron. Where do you think you are now?

But is this home?

It is for now.

Social and material achievements pursued for their own sake are misguided. They serve only the master of the earthly plane. The show of force is a constant reminder of the culture that dominates the conversation: Do or die, become or fade.

Fools who are unwittingly used.

Ignorance persists as wisdom fades.

Stewardship of oneself is as crucial as stewardship of the planet.

Toxic cultures destroy, while healthy cultures preserve.

In the ignorance of the fool, their true nature remains hidden.

When the foundation of reality collapses, the kingdom seeks refuge within.

The collective perception of reality is clouded by the illusion of control.

A broken clock is not correct twice a day, as time itself is an illusion.

Nature and seasons represent natural time.

What about cosmic time?

Every cycle has its purpose.

When the psyche recognizes alternate dimensions, there is a tendency to want to remain in those realms. These dimensions are for exploration only, meant to expand awareness and facilitate understanding. The great mystics have never been fully comprehended. The tendency is often to follow rather than lead. True leadership involves consulting inwardly before external concepts and theories are developed.

You're in a trap!

Yes, I know.

I am trying to exit in the most gentle way possible. It's no one's fault.

Yes, I understand.

No fault, no blame.

Respectable solution?

Emotional boundaries. Support is essential. Embrace and respect the process, but remain firm.

I understand and thank you.